"I DID NOT WANT MY TOMBSTONE TO READ, 'SHE KEPT A REALLY CLEAN HOUSE.' I THINK I'D LIKE THEM TO REMEMBER ME BY SAYING, 'SHE OPENED GOVERNMENT TO EVERYONE.'"

—Ann Richards

FOR ALL OF OUR FOREMOTHERS, ESPECIALLY MY GRANDMOTHERS,
JOYE AND PATRICIA, AND MY MAMA, ANNE —M.P.B.

IN LOVING MEMORY OF MY GRANDMOTHERS —C.W.

Library of Congress Cataloging-in-Publication Data is available upon request.
ISBN 978-0-593-17327-5 (trade) | ISBN 978-0-593-17328-2 (lib. bdg.) | ISBN 978-0-593-17329-9 (ebook)

The text of this book is set in 13-point Century Schoolbook.
The illustrations were rendered in ink and gouache on paper, digitally enhanced.
Book design by Rachael Cole

MANUFACTURED IN CHINA
10 9 8 7 6 5 4 3 2 1
First Edition

INDELIBLE ANN

THE LARGER-THAN-LIFE STORY OF GOVERNOR ANN RICHARDS

BY MEGHAN P. BROWNE

ILLUSTRATED BY CARLYNN WHITT

RANDOM HOUSE STUDIO ⌂ NEW YORK

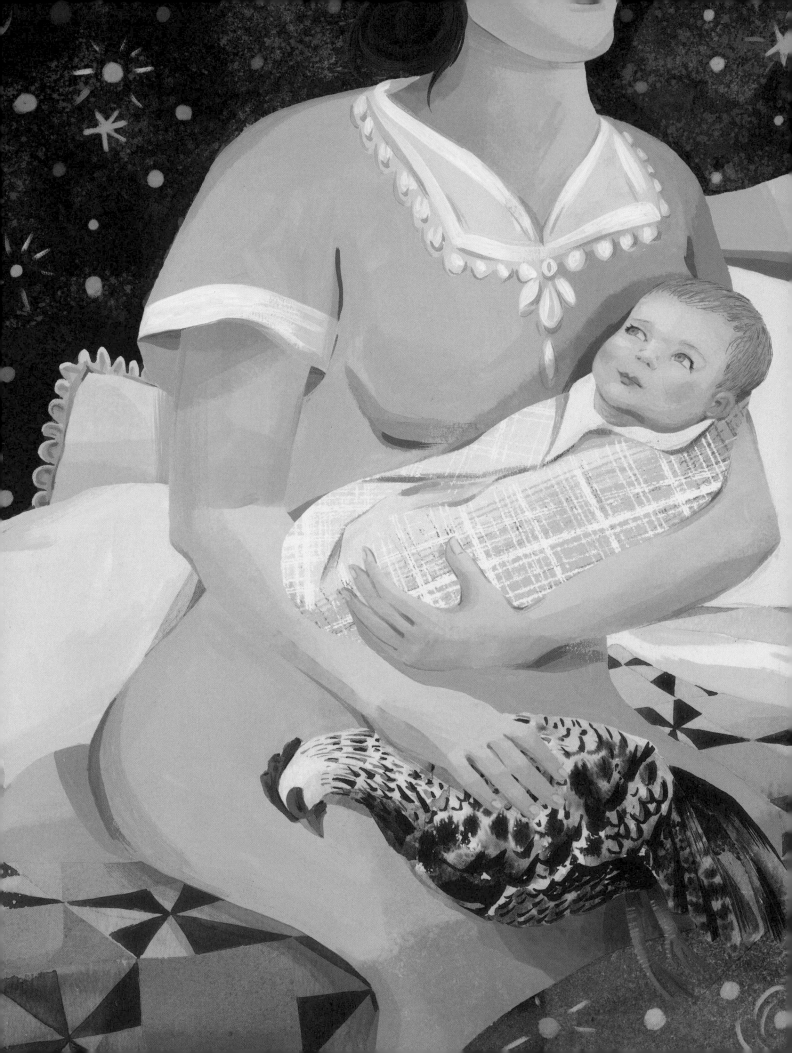

In a tiny wooden farmhouse outside a lonely Texas prairie town, a brand-new mother paused.

Weary from labor pains that felt like barbed wire and anchor chains, she wrung a chicken's neck from her birthing bed. After all, dinner needed fixing, and that was a woman's work, too.

That morning, the universe had opened wide and borne forth a humble heroine fit for a tall tale. She was a baby, all right, but . . .

Dorothy Ann Willis grew up tending chickens and gardens, running down dusty roads until her feet could stand the summer heat, and climbing chinaberry trees. She learned early on how to bait a trotline by the river at dark. She would pedal five miles each way on her bicycle for piano lessons. And by the time Dorothy Ann was in first grade, she performed poems and stories for a packed schoolhouse. That small-town girl had found her voice and the guts to use it.

"You can do anything you'd like in this world," Daddy told her.

"You'll just have to work at it," Mama insisted.

Dorothy Ann wasn't afraid of work. She might have been a bird-legged girl, all right, but . . .

...Just Wait, you'll see.

The war came to the Willis house when Daddy shipped off to California. Mama and Dorothy Ann managed just fine on their own, but Dorothy woke one morning to find that Mama had wrung the neck of every last chicken in the flock. Dorothy Ann helped can the meat, and together they loaded the car to bursting: Daddy was a long way off, but the Willis women were determined to catch up.

San Diego pulsed with life and pushed Dorothy Ann's lens of the world out wide. A streetcar ride over Balboa Park carried her to junior high, where Dorothy Ann's classmates had names and cultures from faraway places. They may have had different backgrounds, all right, but it didn't take long to see just how much they had in common.

When First Lady Eleanor Roosevelt made a surprise visit to the naval hospital in town, she raised a high ruckus by refusing to stop for a reporter's photograph. She couldn't stand the injustice of leaving enlisted Black servicemen out of the frame. Eleanor's boldness excited Dorothy Ann, whose heart had changed forever in California. She might have been a young girl, all right, but . . .

ANN WILLIS

...JUST WAIT, you'll see.

War's end took her family back to Waco, Texas, and the start of high school brought a rising tide deep inside Dorothy Ann. Desperate for a new beginning, she dropped her first name and became Ann.

Ann staked her claim as a speech and debate team marvel. Soon enough, she was on her way to the Capitol for Girls State, a program for young women to learn about government. Ann's experience was more than a lesson in parliamentary procedure. With her outgoing personality, she befriended girls from the citrusy-sweet Rio Grande Valley and the windswept plains of the north Texas panhandle.

The program's director saw the spark of Ann's passion and talent igniting and put her on a train to Washington, DC, to represent Texas at Girls Nation. Young delegates hailing from gleaming cities and far-flung towns across America learned the business of Congress and the importance of civic duty. Their time together ended in the Rose Garden under pop-crackling flashbulbs with a presidential handshake.

Never mind all she had accomplished and learned on her cross-country trip—back home in Waco, news of Ann's friendship with a Black delegate was all anyone could talk about.

While Ann's travels raised chatter and arched eyebrows all over town, one founding member of the Waco League of Women Voters saw potential in the girl's independent spirit. What in the world would it take for her son, David, to be interested in an audacious young woman like *that*? Ann might have been a starry-eyed teenager, all right, but . . .

...JUST WAIT, you'll see.

When they finally met, David and Ann were inseparable. They inspired each other, challenged each other, made each other laugh. With college graduation soon behind them, Ann and David married and filled their house with political activists—and four children.

Many years at the University of Motherhood taught Ann stamina for never-ending workdays, grit in advocating for her children, and coordination to juggle it all. It wasn't long before Ann's patience for answering phones and sending mailers as a political volunteer ran bone-dry. There were people to meet and problems that needed fixing. Ann knew this was a woman's work, too.

She might have been a perfect housewife, all right, but . . .

PENNYBACKER BRIDGE

JUST WAIT,
... you'll see.

Ann stood up and raised her helping hand high. Though women hadn't often been trusted with the kind of responsibility that came with public office, Ann convinced voters that time was ripe for change. She earned her place as county commissioner and built a bridge between the predictable past and the limitless future.

But even earthshakers like Ann need help now and again. The life she'd taken such care to create began to crumble, and Ann's marriage could not survive the strain. Family and friends held Ann up until she regained her footing, her strength, and that stem-winding voice.

Ann was elected state treasurer and hardly had time to be surprised. The treasury was bogged down with scandal. She set to hiring a hardworking staff that reflected the folks around her. If children could see people who looked like their parents working at the Capitol, Ann thought, they could imagine their own future there.

Ann's team digitized the treasury: instead of having to wait for paper checks by mail, people could get payments by computer faster than a prairie fire with a tailwind. Every second saved kept money in the pockets of Texans toiling to make ends meet. Ann's star had risen high, all right, but . . .

...JUST WAIT, you'll see.

One sweltering summer night in Atlanta, Georgia, the lights went down on a roaring national convention. The hall stilled. And when those lights came back up, a high-cotton-haired Ann Richards dazzled the crowd and delighted television viewers everywhere. Her one-liners zinged. Her Southern drawl zanged. Just as soon as Ann finished making everyone laugh till they cried, folks asked why *Ann* wasn't running for president.

ERA YES!

ANN!

Because there was still work to be done in Texas.

Ann stood up and raised her helping hand high again, this time to run for governor. It was an uphill campaign, spattered with muddy attacks and stinging insults.

A whole mess of Texans thought Ann was out of her league and destined for defeat.

But Ann couldn't be stopped. She kept on visiting all those little towns. She steered a boat through coastal waterways. She listened to the people: a colorful patchwork of Texans sewn tightly together by their desire for change. . . .

And when they elected her the forty-fifth
governor of Texas, they joined hands, marched
up Congress Avenue, and took back the Capitol
for the people, just like Ann had promised.

Governor Richards believed in doing the right thing no matter what, taking care of *all* people, and working together. Ann spoke up for those whose voices had long been ignored, made laws to protect the land, and empowered teachers in every corner of the Lone Star State. She whipped words into speeches that inspired teamwork and brought along those standing in the way. A new day had come with Ann's rise.

Ann's governorship ended in a reelection loss, but her work kept right on. There were changes to make, people to empower, wrongs to right. And that was a woman's work, too.

A Woman's Place Is in the Dome!

With all of Ann's words delivered, and her life complete, many wondered—will we ever see such greatness again? After all, Ann was her own tall tale. Larger than life, nearly unbelievable, but oh, my . . . undeniably indelible.

MORE ABOUT ANN RICHARDS

Briscoe Center, UT-Austin

Twelve-year-old Ann Willis and the bike that took her around Lakeview, Texas.

Dorothy "Ann" Willis Richards, the forty-fifth governor of Texas, was born on September 1, 1933, in Lakeview, a small town just outside of Waco. The Willis family—and all Americans—were in the midst of surviving the worst year of the decade-long Great Depression. Ann's parents taught their only child self-sufficiency and hard work in the face of adversity.

Despite the circumstances, Ann's upbringing in Texas was mostly idyllic. It wasn't until her family moved to California that she realized just how big the world was outside her small Texas hometown. At the end of World War II, her father was drafted into the Navy and deployed to San Diego, and Ann and her mother followed. In the city by the sea, Ann lived in a culturally diverse community for the first time in her life. That experience forever changed her perspective.

Societal expectations led Ann to follow the path of many women of that era: marriage, childbearing, and homemaking. Ann married David Richards, a burgeoning civil rights attorney. The two became active members of the Democratic Party and had four children before settling in Austin, the capital of Texas, in 1969.

In the 1970s, Ann cut her political teeth managing the campaigns of up-and-coming female leaders, and shortly after made her own seat at the table. She became the first woman elected Travis County Commissioner in 1976.

As professional demands increased, Ann's personal life began to falter. Ann struggled with an addiction to alcohol that strained her family life and friendships. In 1980, Ann sought outpatient treatment for the disease and began a life of sobriety that would last the rest of her days. Ann's thirty-year marriage to David ended in 1984.

In 1988, Ann was returning calls at an airport pay phone when the Democratic National Committee Chairman asked her to deliver a nationally televised keynote speech at the Democratic National Convention ahead of the presidential election. Though she could hardly believe her ears, Ann took on the challenge. During her address, Ann spoke plainly, spoke her mind, and made folks laugh—sometimes at her own expense. Her speech was a rip-roaring success, and she came back to Texas with the kind of name recognition that made her an obvious choice for a gubernatorial candidate.

The 1990 contest for governor of Texas was hard-fought. Ann ran against wealthy West Texas oilman Clayton "Claytie" Williams, who slung words carelessly, while Ann stood her ground in Texas town squares. Voters elected Ann Richards to the highest office that year.

Governor Ann Richards reformed a broken prison system, championed civil rights for LGBTQ and minority communities, and advocated for educational equity. She changed the face of Texas politics forever by appointing highly qualified people from diverse backgrounds to leadership positions. Governor Richards knew that once the doors to government were open to all people, they could never be closed.

Though she lost her reelection campaign to George W. Bush in 1994, Ann continued to be involved in politics nationwide. In the same way she felt inspired early in life by First Lady Eleanor Roosevelt's fight for equality, Ann Richards used her national stage to champion equal rights even as throat cancer began stealing her stem-winding voice. Governor Richards's work blazed the trail for many other women in politics and activism, including her own daughter, Cecile Richards. Ann Richards died on September 13, 2006, at the age of seventy-three, but her legacy lives on in those who seek to make the world better for all.

SELECTED SOURCES

"Ann W. Richards." *Portraits of Texas Governors | Modern Texas*, Texas State Library and Archives Commission, Dec. 3, 2015, tsl.texas.gov/governors/modern/page3.html#Richards.

Patterson, Keith, and Phillip Schopper, directors. *All About Ann: Governor Richards of the Lone Star State*. HBO, 2014.

Reid, Jan. *Let the People In: The Life and Times of Ann Richards*. Austin: University of Texas Press, 2014.

Richards, Ann. *Straight from the Heart*. New York: Simon and Schuster, 1989.

Richards, Cecile. *Make Trouble: Standing Up, Speaking Out, and Finding the Courage to Lead*. New York: Gallery Books, 2018.

Texas Governor-Elect Ann Richards celebrates her election night win, November 7, 1990.

First Lady Hillary Clinton, Governor Ann Richards, and former First Lady, Lady Bird Johnson at the Liz Carpenter Lectureship Series, UT-Austin, April 7, 1993.

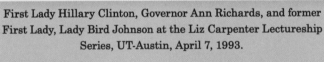

Governor Ann Richards celebrating her 60th birthday on a Harley under the Capitol Rotunda in Austin, 1993.

"WE'RE NOT GOING TO HAVE THE AMERICA THAT WE WANT UNTIL WE ELECT LEADERS WHO ARE GOING TO TELL THE TRUTH— NOT MOST DAYS, BUT EVERY DAY."

—Ann Richards